Doctor Mozart® Music ~

In-Depth Piano Theory Fun for Children's

g

Level 2B - Partial Contents

Every day, start ... you learned the day before. Then complete just one or two exercises, or even a full page. Do this daily and you will make good progress.

Highly Effective for Beginners Learning a Musical Instrument.

Doctor Mozart workbooks are filled with friendly cartoon characters. They make it fun to learn music theory in-depth. And in-depth music theory knowledge is essential for children learning a musical instrument. Use Doctor Mozart workbooks by themselves or with other teaching materials. Use them for music lessons and for home schooling.

The authors, Machiko and Paul Musgrave, are both graduates of Juilliard. Machiko has taught piano and theory at Soai University in Japan. Paul is an Associate of the Royal Conservatory of Music. The authors hope you enjoy using this book!

Many thanks to Kevin Musgrave for his meticulous proof-reading and insightful suggestions.

Created by Machiko and Paul Christopher Musgrave. Illustrated by Machiko Yamane Musgrave.   1.0.5

Where Should You Go Next?

Here are some signs that can help you find your way when reading music.

Da capo al fine means _____ to the _____ of the music. End at the word _____.

The above marks indicate the _____ and _____ endings.

D.S. means: _____ from the _____

Doctor Mozart Music Theory Workbook, Level 2B.   © MMVIII, MMXII Machiko and Paul Christopher Musgrave.   Published by April Avenue Music.   www.DoctorMozart.com   800 567-8878

Step Over the Cat?

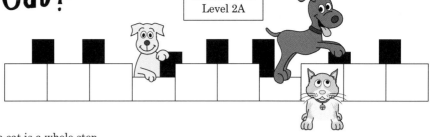

Review from
Level 2A

Below, mark each half
step with a V bracket.
Mark each whole step
with a square bracket.

Each paw print pair that steps past a cat is a whole step.

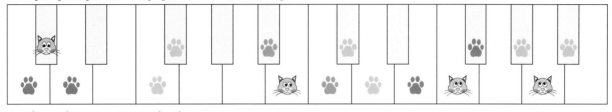

Find a *half* step *above* each paw print, and mark that note with a letter H – for half step.
Find a *whole* step *above* each paw print, and mark that note with a letter W – for whole step.

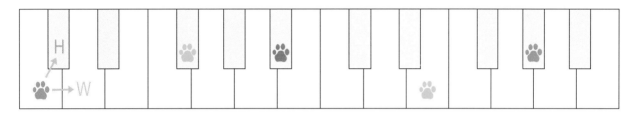

Find a *half* step *below* each paw print, and mark that note with a letter H.
Find a *whole* step *below* each paw print, and mark that note with a letter W.

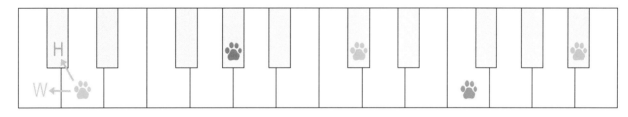

Draw lines from notes to keys. Mark each half step with a V bracket. Mark
each whole step with a square bracket. Remember, bar lines cancel accidentals.

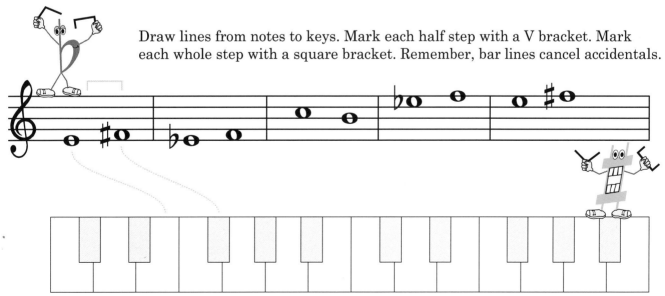

Doctor Mozart Music Theory Workbook, Level 2B.   © MMVIII, MMXII Machiko and Paul Christopher Musgrave.   Published by April Avenue Music.   www.DoctorMozart.com   800 567-8878

White Key Sharps and Flats

Trace the letters

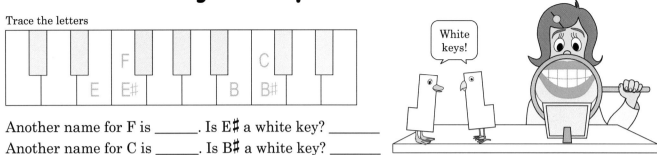

Another name for F is _____. Is E♯ a white key? _____

Another name for C is _____. Is B♯ a white key? _____

Below, label each E♯ and B♯ on the keyboard. Write the notes on the staff. Draw lines.

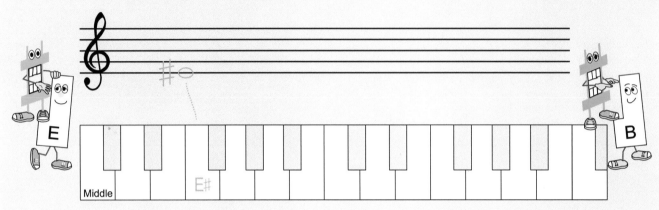

Trace the letters

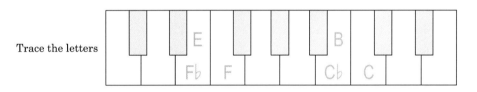

Another name for E is _____. Is F♭ a white key? _____

Another name for B is _____. Is C♭ a white key? _____

Below, label each F♭ and C♭ on the keyboard. Write the notes on the staff. Draw lines.

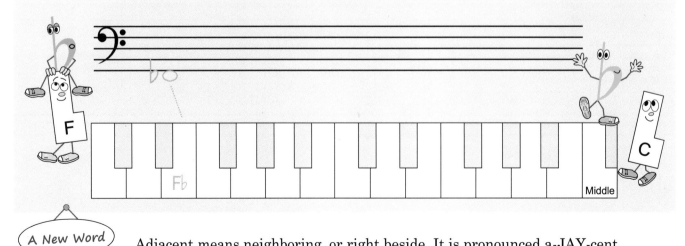

A New Word Adjacent means neighboring, or right beside. It is pronounced a-JAY-cent.

Another word for neighboring is a_____. We will use this word often.

Doctor Mozart Music Theory Workbook, Level 2B.   © MMVIII, MMXII Machiko and Paul Christopher Musgrave.   Published by April Avenue Music.   www.DoctorMozart.com   800 567-8878

Enharmonics

Enharmonic equivalents are two different names for a single note on the keyboard.

Review

Write two names for each white key that has colored boxes. Write the notes on the staff. Draw lines to the keys.

Use natural signs to cancel any preceding accidentals.

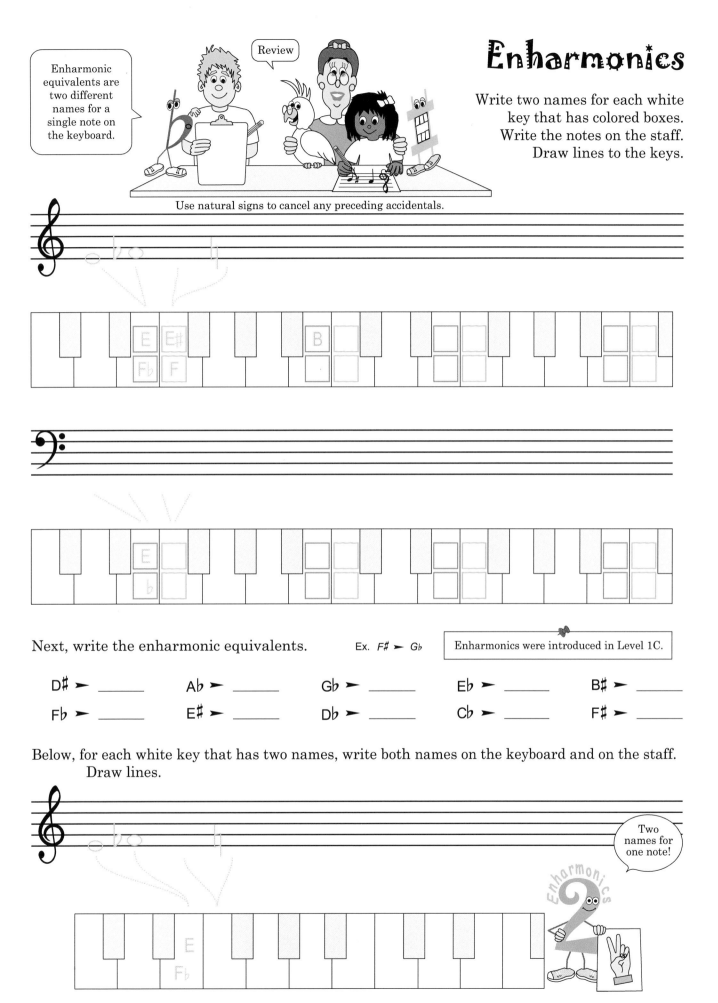

Next, write the enharmonic equivalents.   Ex. F♯ ➤ G♭   Enharmonics were introduced in Level 1C.

D♯ ➤ _____   A♭ ➤ _____   G♭ ➤ _____   E♭ ➤ _____   B♯ ➤ _____

F♭ ➤ _____   E♯ ➤ _____   D♭ ➤ _____   C♭ ➤ _____   F♯ ➤ _____

Below, for each white key that has two names, write both names on the keyboard and on the staff. Draw lines.

Two names for one note!

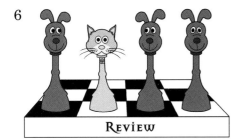

Review

Whole & Half Step Test

Chromatic half steps are written with just *one* letter name.

Diatonic half steps are written with _____ adjacent letter names. Draw lines from notes to keys. Write CH above every chromatic half step. Write DH above every diatonic half step.

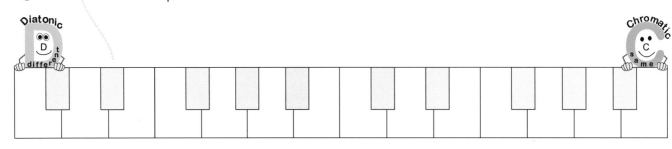

Remember, bar lines cancel accidentals.

Next, trace the clef. Write these whole steps two different ways on the bass staff. Draw lines.

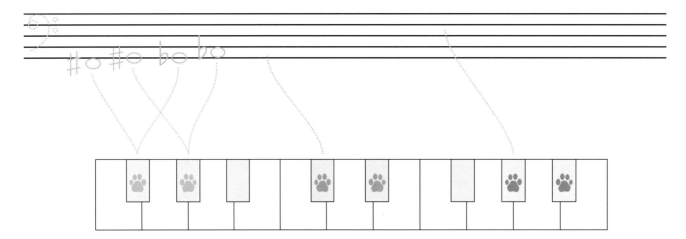

Trace the clef. Beside each note, write its enharmonic equivalent. Draw lines to the keyboard.

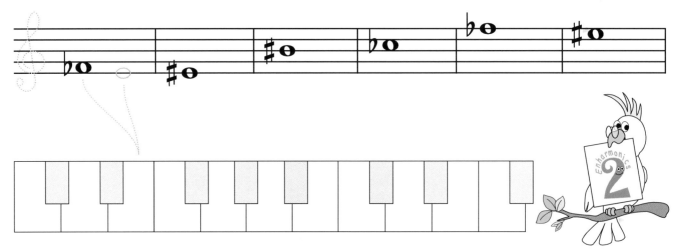

Doctor Mozart Music Theory Workbook, Level 2B.   © MMVIII, MMXII Machiko and Paul Christopher Musgrave.   Published by April Avenue Music.   www.DoctorMozart.com   800 567-8878

Enharmonic Whole Steps

Name these whole steps two
different ways on the keyboard,
and on the staff. Follow the
direction of the arrows.

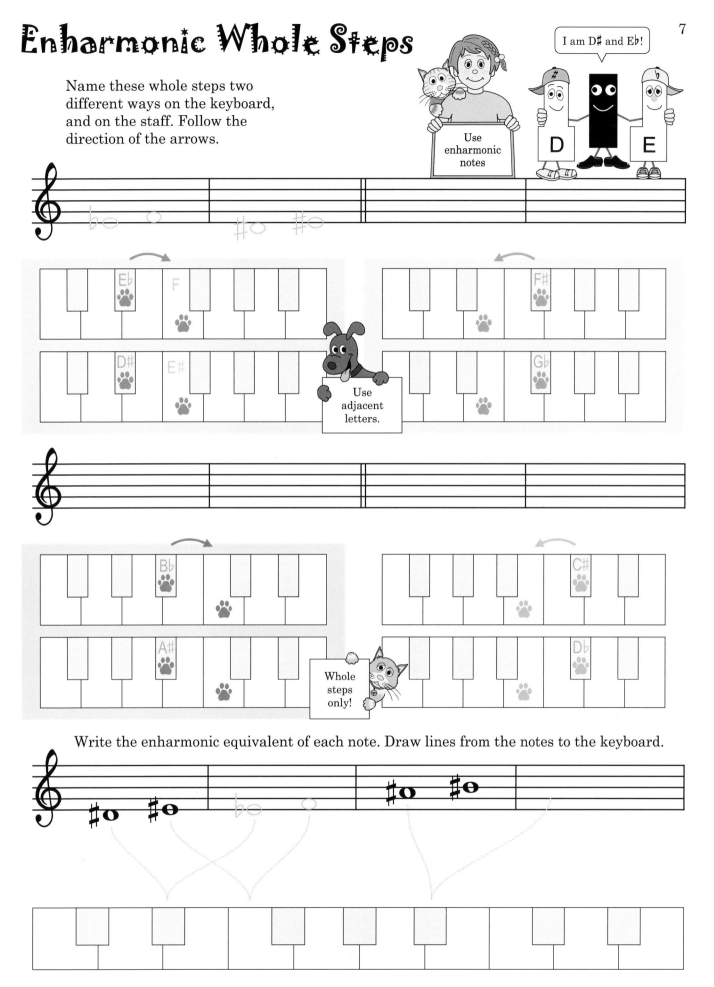

I am D# and E♭!

Use
enharmonic
notes

Use
adjacent
letters.

Whole
steps
only!

Write the enharmonic equivalent of each note. Draw lines from the notes to the keyboard.

A Major 2nd is a Whole Step.

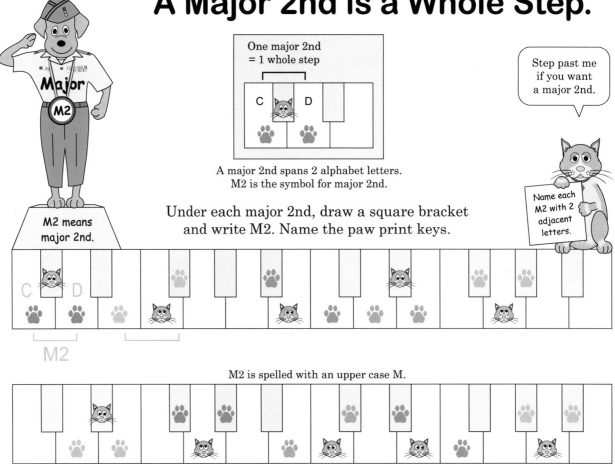

One major 2nd = 1 whole step

A major 2nd spans 2 alphabet letters.
M2 is the symbol for major 2nd.

Step past me if you want a major 2nd.

Name each M2 with 2 adjacent letters.

Under each major 2nd, draw a square bracket and write M2. Name the paw print keys.

M2 means major 2nd.

M2 is spelled with an upper case M.

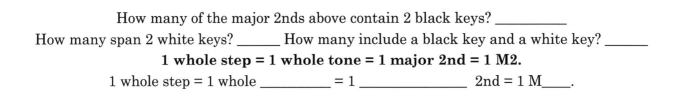

How many of the major 2nds above contain 2 black keys? _____

How many span 2 white keys? _____ How many include a black key and a white key? _____

1 whole step = 1 whole tone = 1 major 2nd = 1 M2.

1 whole step = 1 whole _____ = 1 _____ 2nd = 1 M____.

Next, write these major 2nds on the staff. Follow the direction of the arrows.
Use adjacent letters. Draw lines.

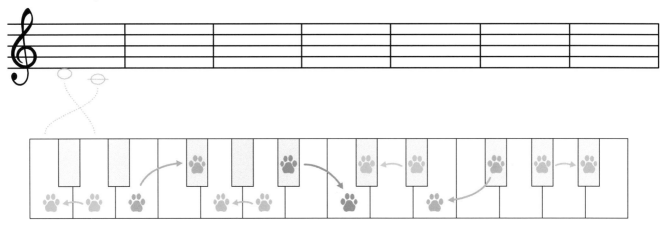

Major 2nd Quiz

Write each major 2nd on the staff.
Follow the direction of the arrows.
Use adjacent letters. Draw lines.

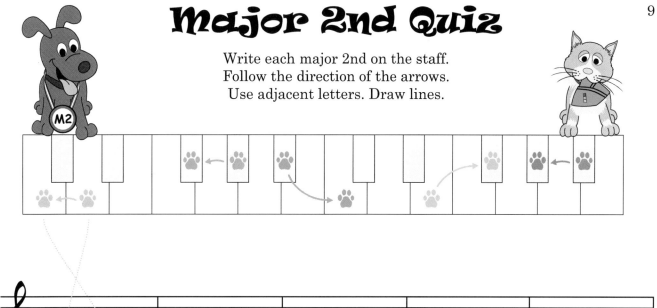

After each note, write a major 2nd. Follow the direction of the arrows.

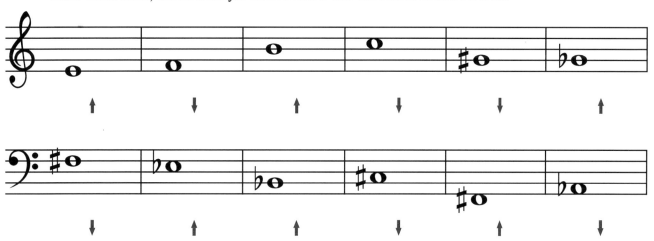

Below, write some major 2nds. Make some go up, and others go down.
Include some black keys and ledger notes. Draw lines from notes to keys.

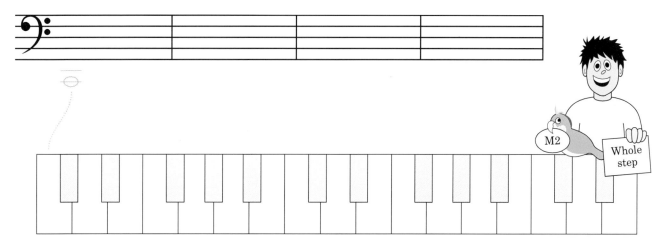

How to Measure Intervals

An interval is the distance between two notes. A major 2nd is a kind of i_____.

An interval is the distance between two _____.

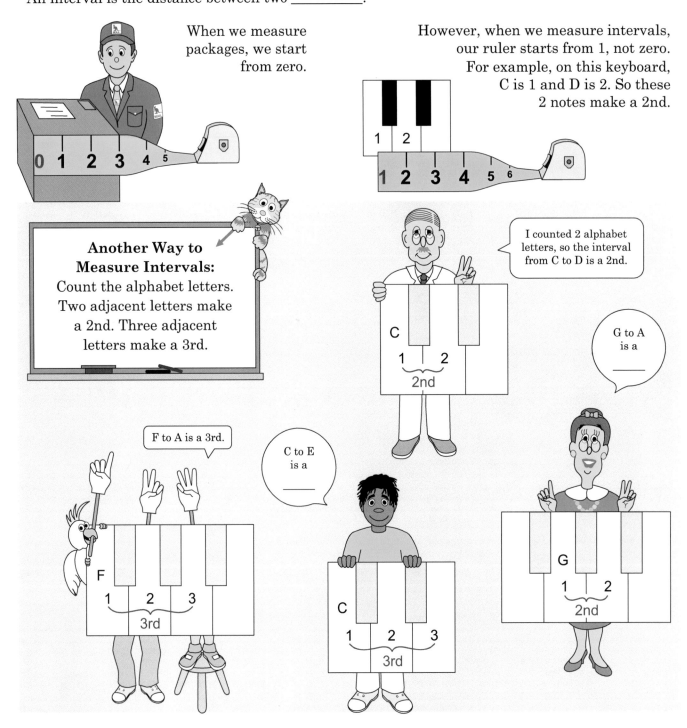

Number the keys spanned by each bracket. Name the intervals.

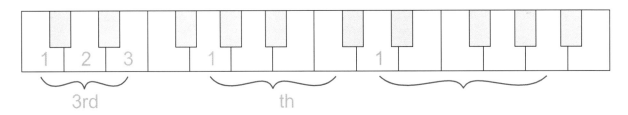

Doctor Mozart Music Theory Workbook, Level 2B.   © MMVIII, MMXII Machiko and Paul Christopher Musgrave.   Published by April Avenue Music.   www.DoctorMozart.com   800 567-8878

A Minor 2nd is Smaller

One minor 2nd
= one half step

Db

C

A minor 2nd spans
2 alphabet letters

Trace the brackets at left. Is a *minor 2nd* smaller than a major 2nd? _____
One diatonic half step = one ___mi_____ 2nd = one m2.

Below, label each minor 2nd with m2 and
a V bracket. Label each major 2nd with
M2 and a square bracket. Name the paw
print keys. Use adjacent alphabet letters.

A minor
2nd is a
diatonic
half step.

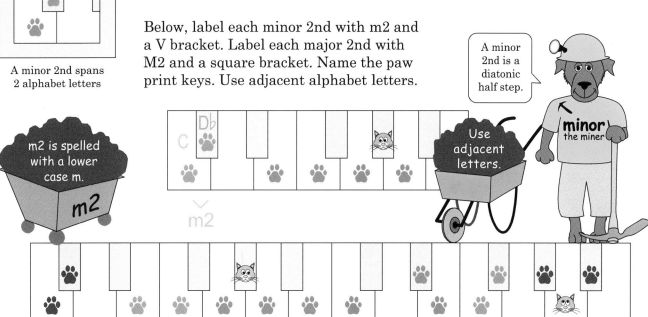

m2 is spelled
with a lower
case m.

m2

Use
adjacent
letters.

minor
the miner

How many minor 2nds did you find above that contain 2 black keys? _____
How many span 2 white keys? _____ How many include a black key and a white key? _____
1 diatonic half step = 1 diatonic semitone = 1 minor 2nd = 1 m2.
1 diatonic half step = 1 diatonic _____ = 1 _____ 2nd = 1 _____.

Next, write these minor 2nds on the staff. Use adjacent alphabet letters. Follow the direction
of the arrows. Draw lines from notes to keys.

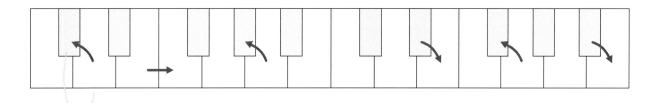

One minor 2nd = 1 _d_____ semitone = one ___2. Why is a *chromatic* semitone not a
minor 2nd? Because its two notes are named with just one alphabet letter. Is the interval A to A♯
a minor 2nd? _____. It is not a minor 2nd, because its notes are named with just one letter.

Adjacent Letters for Minor 2nds

Write a minor 2nd in each pair of boxes. Write the notes on the staff. Follow the direction of the arrows. Draw lines.

Below, name the notes. Draw lines. Write m2 above each minor 2nd.
Write CH above each chromatic half step.

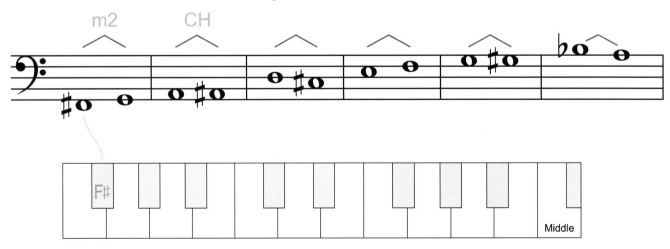

Major & Minor 2nd Quiz

Every 2nd is made with

two _a_____
alphabet letters.

Below, at each major 2nd, circle
the Major's hat. At each minor 2nd,
circle the miner's hat.

Below, write three different minor 2nds, and three different major 2nds. Make some go up, and others go down. Use notes of various different lengths. Draw lines from notes to keys. At each 2nd, write M2 or m2. Draw square and V brackets.

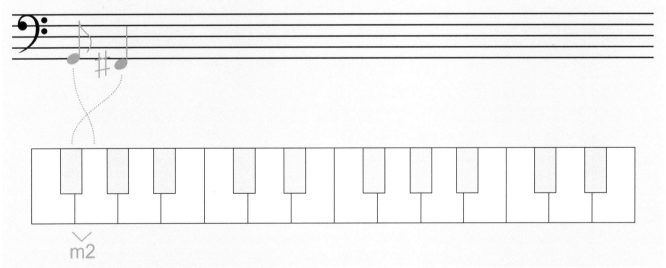

Next, write major and minor 2nds, as indicated by the hats and arrows.

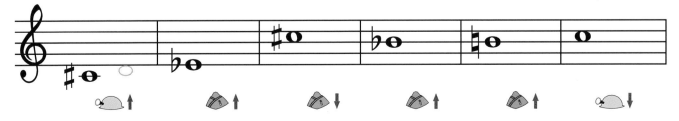

Doctor Mozart Music Theory Workbook, Level 2B.   © MMVIII, MMXII Machiko and Paul Christopher Musgrave.   Published by April Avenue Music.   www.DoctorMozart.com   800 567-8878

Time, Terms, & Enharmonics Review

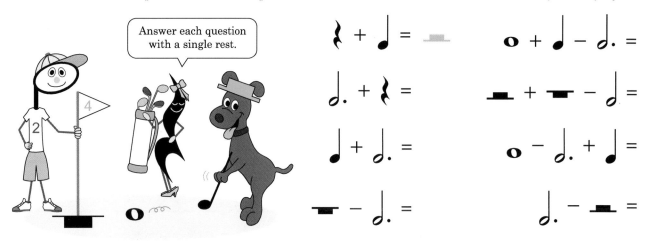

Answer each question with a single rest.

Draw lines to match each term or sign with its meaning. Some lines may go to the same place.

|1. |2.

Da capo al fine

D.S.

Dal segno

D.C. al fine

𝄋

Repeat from the sign.

Repeat from the beginning, and end at the word *fine*.

Segno, which means sign.

First and second endings.

Draw lines to match each rest with a note of the same length.

Write the enharmonic equivalent of each note. Draw lines from the notes to the keyboard.

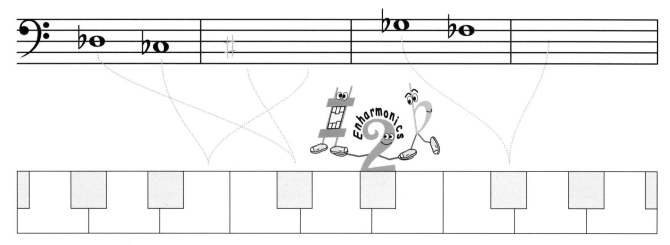

Eighths at Rest

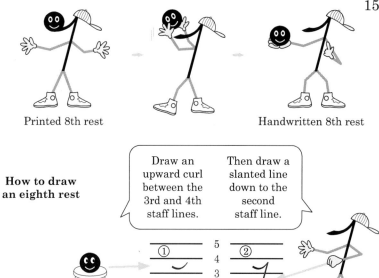

Printed 8th rest   Handwritten 8th rest

How to draw an eighth rest

Draw an upward curl between the 3rd and 4th staff lines.

Then draw a slanted line down to the second staff line.

This is an eighth rest. It means you should stay silent for the length of an eighth note.

Below, trace the eighth rests. Then draw 6 more.

Complete these sums.

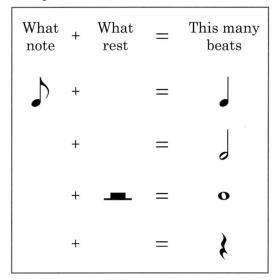

What note	+	What rest	=	This many beats

Below, draw lines to match the rests, the notes, and the number of beats.

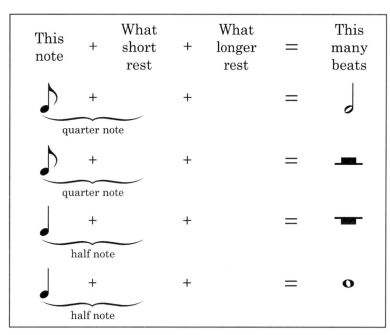

This note	+	What short rest	+	What longer rest	=	This many beats

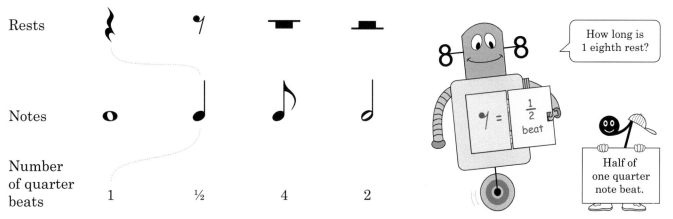

Rests

Notes

Number of quarter beats   1   ½   4   2

How long is 1 eighth rest?

Half of one quarter note beat.

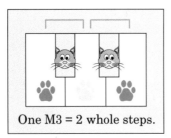

Pass 2 Cats for a Major 3rd

One M3 = 2 whole steps.

M3 is the symbol for major 3rd.
The upper case M means major.

Trace the gray brackets at left. Two major
seconds together make a major 3rd, or M3.
A major 3rd equals two ___m_____ 2nds.
A major 3rd also equals two ___w_____ steps.
To make a major 3rd, we pass _____ cats.

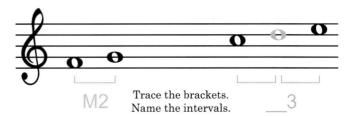

Neighbors   Not neighbors

What note is 2 whole steps above C? _____.
C to E is a _____ 3rd, or M3.
The symbol for major 3rd is M___.

The 2 notes in
a major 3rd are
not neighbors.
They span 3
alphabet letters.

M2   Trace the brackets.
            Name the intervals.   ___3

Below, number the bracketed keys. Name the intervals. Write them on the staff. Draw lines.

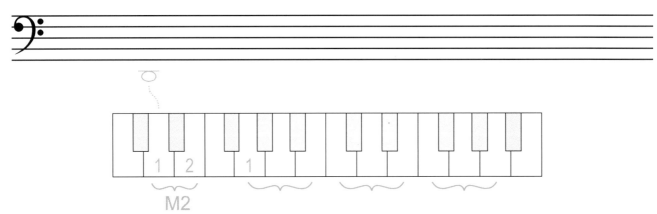

M2

Write some major 3rds on the keyboard and on the staff. Draw lines and square brackets.

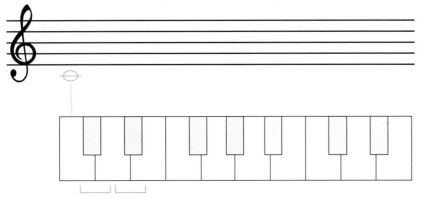

CATS & DOGS CHESS CO.

Doctor Mozart Music Theory Workbook, Level 2B.   © MMVIII, MMXII Machiko and Paul Christopher Musgrave.   Published by April Avenue Music.   www.DoctorMozart.com   800 567-8878

Write adjacent letters in the boxes. In each case, name the white keys first. Write the 3rds on the staff. Draw lines and square brackets.

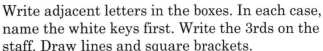

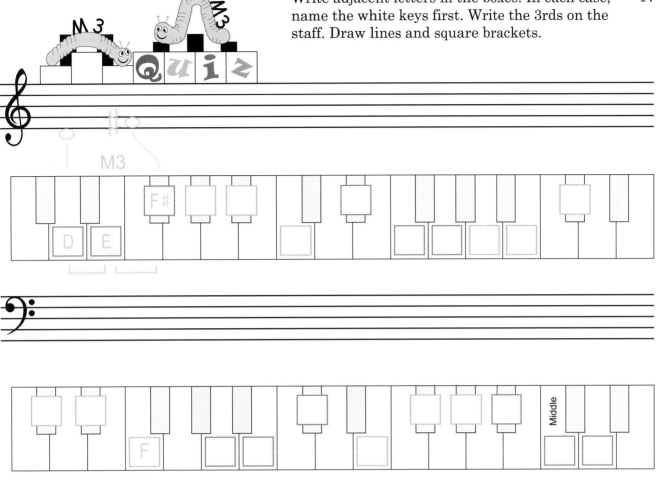

Above each paw print, write a major 3rd on the keyboard and the staff . Draw lines and brackets.

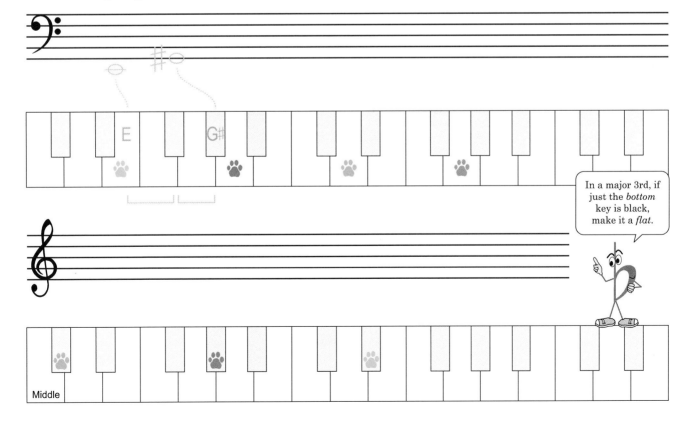

In a major 3rd, if just the *bottom* key is black, make it a *flat*.

Doctor Mozart Music Theory Workbook, Level 2B.   © MMVIII, MMXII Machiko and Paul Christopher Musgrave.   Published by April Avenue Music.   www.DoctorMozart.com   800 567-8878

Major 3rds Up and Down

You can count up from the lower key, or count down from the higher key.

Count in both directions
⇄
on the keyboard

You can also count up or down on the staff.

Count in both directions
↑↓
on the staff

Name the intervals. Draw lines.

M3   M3

1 2 3   3 2 1

Name the paw print keys. Name the intervals. Write them on the staff. Draw lines.

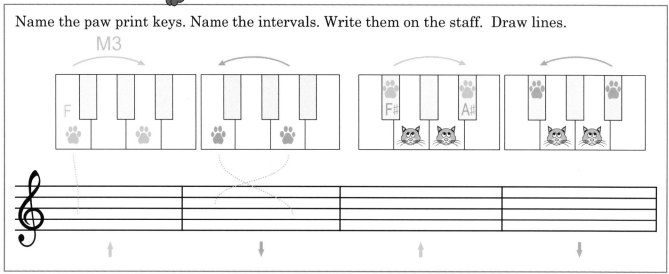

M3

F   F#   A#

Name the intervals. Write them on the staff. Follow the direction of the arrows. Draw lines.

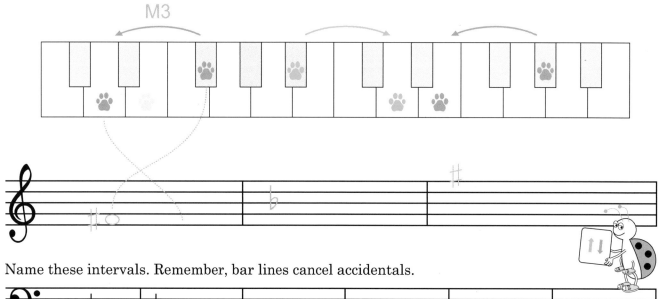

M3

Name these intervals. Remember, bar lines cancel accidentals.

m2

Doctor Mozart Music Theory Workbook, Level 2B.   © MMVIII, MMXII Machiko and Paul Christopher Musgrave.   Published by April Avenue Music.   www.DoctorMozart.com   800 567-8878

A Minor 3rd is Smaller

One minor 3rd (m3)

Trace the gray brackets at left.
1 minor 3rd equals
1 whole step + one h_____ step.

Below, write adjacent alphabet letters
in the boxes to show minor 3rds.
Draw square and V brackets.

M2 + m2 = m3 minor the miner

m3 is spelled with a lower case m.

What note is 1 whole step + 1 half step above C? _____. What note is 1 whole step + 1 half step above F? _____. Each of these intervals is a minor 3rd, or m3. A minor 3rd is the same as one _____ step plus one _____ step. It is the same as 1 M2 + 1 m____.

1 whole step + 1 half step

Below, draw square and V brackets to show the minor 3rds. Write the minor thirds on the staff. Draw lines from notes to keys.

Next, write a minor 3rd above each given note on the staff.
Draw square and V brackets. Draw lines to the keyboard.

Doctor Mozart Music Theory Workbook, Level 2B.   © MMVIII, MMXII Machiko and Paul Christopher Musgrave.   Published by April Avenue Music.   www.DoctorMozart.com   800 567-8878

20

Write adjacent letters in the boxes. In each case, name the white keys first. Write the 3rds on the staff. Draw lines and square brackets.

Write a minor 3rd above each paw print, on the keyboard and on the staff. Draw brackets.

In a minor 3rd, if just the *bottom* key is black, make it a *sharp*.

In a minor 3rd, if the bottom and top keys are *both* black, make them both flat or both sharp.

M3 or m3?

Under each bracket, write M3 for major 3rd, or m3 for minor 3rd.

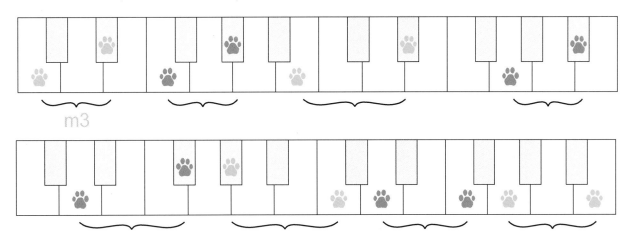

Under each pair of paw prints, draw square and V brackets. Write M3 or m3. Write the 3rds on the staff. Draw lines from notes to keys.

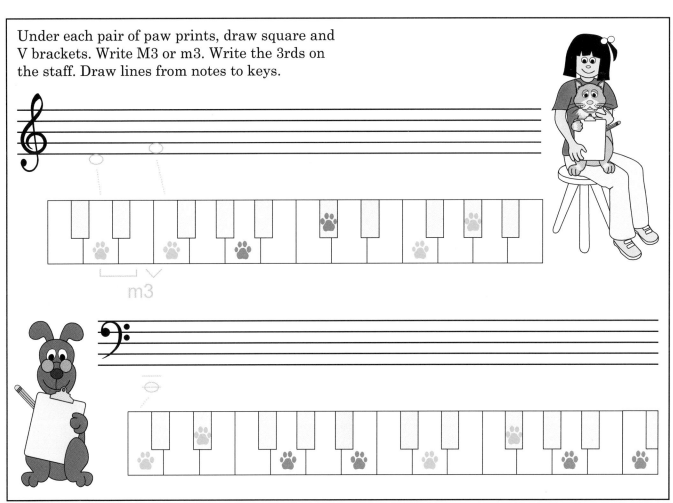

Under each bracket, write M3 or m3.

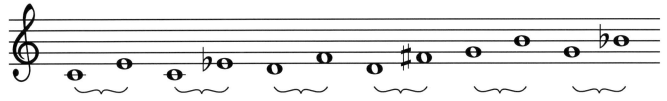

22

Tapping Eighths

Tap this rhythm, hands together, while counting the beats aloud. Repeat the rhythm until you can tap it well.

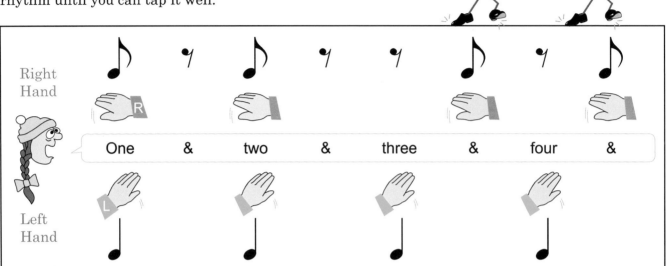

If the bottom number in a time signature is 8, then each beat is one 8th note long.
Below, number the beats. Write any 8th rests needed to complete each bar.
Tap each rhythm, hands together, while counting aloud. Repeat until perfect.

Doctor Mozart Music Theory Workbook, Level 2B.   © MMVIII, MMXII Machiko and Paul Christopher Musgrave.   Published by April Avenue Music.   www.DoctorMozart.com   800 567-8878

Measure Your Rests

Number the beats. Write an ampersand (&) under any note or rest that is between the beats. Draw the bar lines. Tap while counting.

Write a single rest at each X. Number the beats.

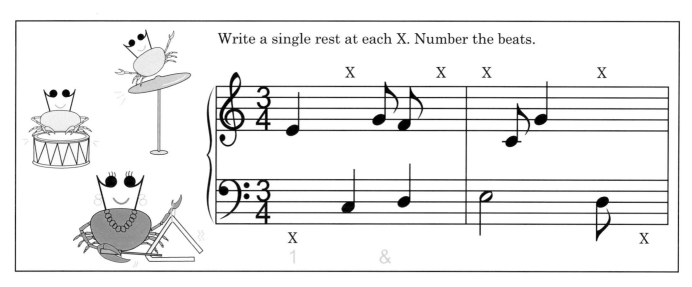

Next, make a grand staff and a 4/4 time signature. Write any half, quarter, and eighth notes and rests you like. Include some ledger notes. Number the beats. Tap and count.

Doctor Mozart Music Theory Workbook, Level 2B.   © MMVIII, MMXII Machiko and Paul Christopher Musgrave.   Published by April Avenue Music.   www.DoctorMozart.com   800 567-8878

Convert Major 3rds to Minor 3rds

A major 3rd is made with two _____ steps. A minor 3rd is made with one _____
step and one _____ step. A _____ 3rd is larger than a _____ 3rd. Can you
convert a major 3rd into a minor 3rd? Yes you can! Just make the major 3rd one half step
smaller. You can do that by lowering the top note.

To convert a
major 3rd to a
minor 3rd ...

Major
M3

minor m3
the miner

... lower the
top note by
1 half step.

Draw red arrows to show how each
right paw print should move to
make a minor 3rd. Then write each
minor 3rd on the staff. Draw lines.

Lower the
top notes to
make minor
3rds.

Major

Middle

Convert Minor 3rds to Major 3rds

You can convert a minor 3rd into a major 3rd. Just make the
minor 3rd one half step larger. To do that, raise the top note.

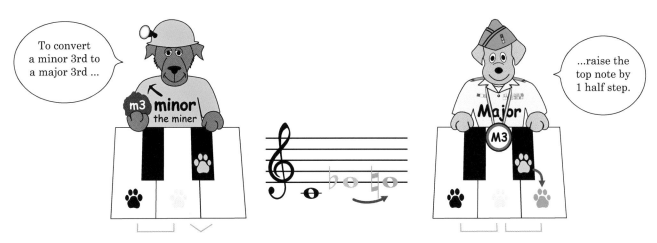

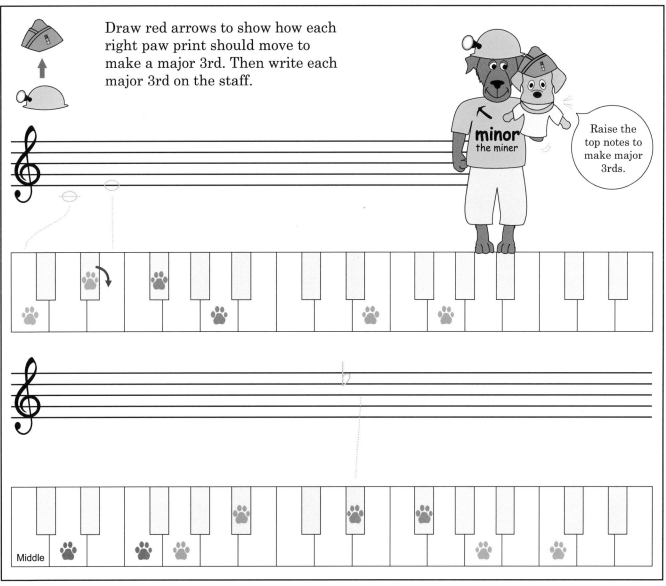

Doctor Mozart Music Theory Workbook, Level 2B.   © MMVIII, MMXII Machiko and Paul Christopher Musgrave.   Published by April Avenue Music.   www.DoctorMozart.com   800 567-8878

2 Ways to Make a Minor 3rd

minor 3rd

A whole step and a half step,

or a half step and a whole step.

You can make a minor 3rd by starting with a whole step – or by starting with a half step. A whole step plus a half step gets you to the same place as a half step plus a whole step.

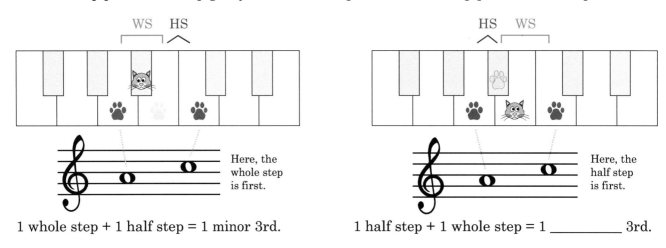

WS   HS

Here, the whole step is first.

1 whole step + 1 half step = 1 minor 3rd.

HS   WS

Here, the half step is first.

1 half step + 1 whole step = 1 _____ 3rd.

In each colored box, count to a minor 3rd two different ways. Number the keys to show how.

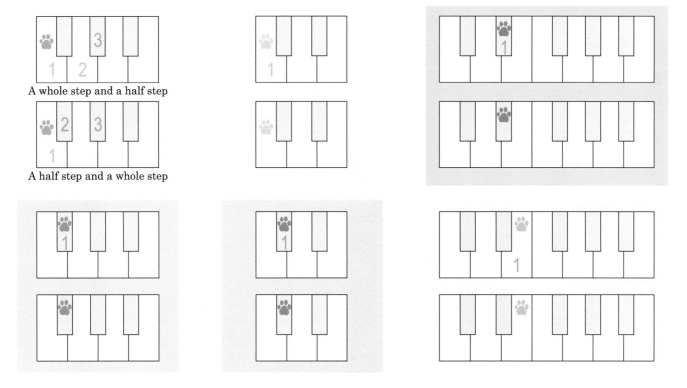

A whole step and a half step

A half step and a whole step

Major & Minor 3rd Quiz

Write the intervals indicated, up from each given note.
Draw lines to the keys. Name the keys.

Number the lower keyboard so that the half step comes first in each m3. Draw brackets.

Below, make the minor 3rds major, and make the major 3rds minor. Draw lines to the keys.

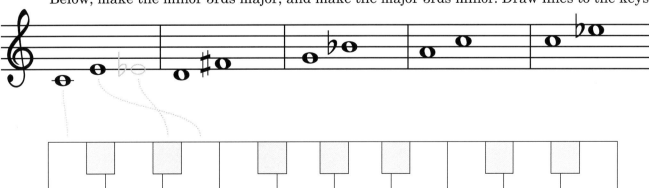

Doctor Mozart Music Theory Workbook, Level 2B. © MMVIII, MMXII Machiko and Paul Christopher Musgrave. Published by April Avenue Music. www.DoctorMozart.com 800 567-8878

Sharp or Flat?

If a 3rd contains a black key, is it easier to write it with a sharp or a flat? Look at this table to find out.

Sharp or flat? How to decide.	If the **bottom** note is black:	If the **top** note is black:	If **both** notes are black:
Major 3rd	Make it ♭	Make it ♯	Make both ♯ or both ♭
Minor 3rd	Make it ♯	Make it ♭	

These are *not* rules. These are suggestions to help make writing 3rds *easy*.

Look at the hats. Then make a 3rd *above* each colored key as shown. Draw connecting arrows.

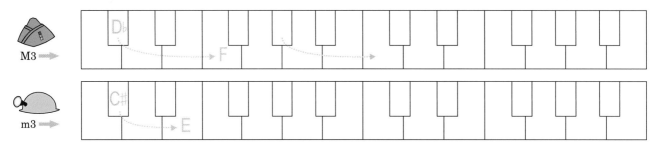

Look at the hats. Then make a 3rd *below* each colored key as shown. Draw connecting arrows.

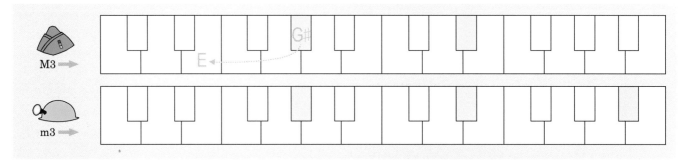

Name each interval. Draw lines to the keys. Remember, bar lines cancel accidentals.

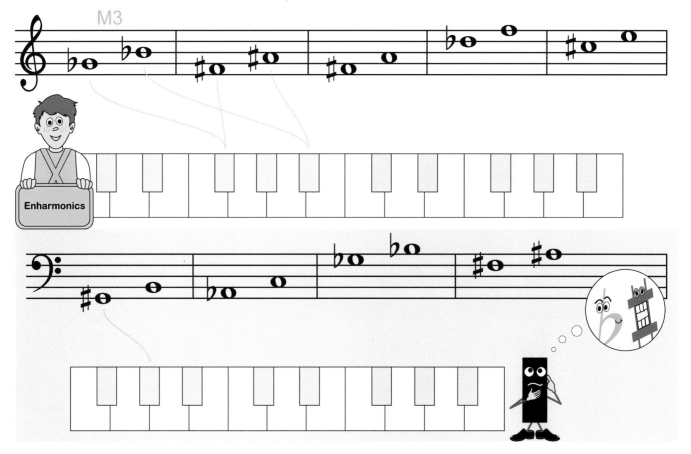

Major 3rds Up and Down Quiz

On the staff and keyboard, write a major 3rd *down* from each paw print. Draw lines.

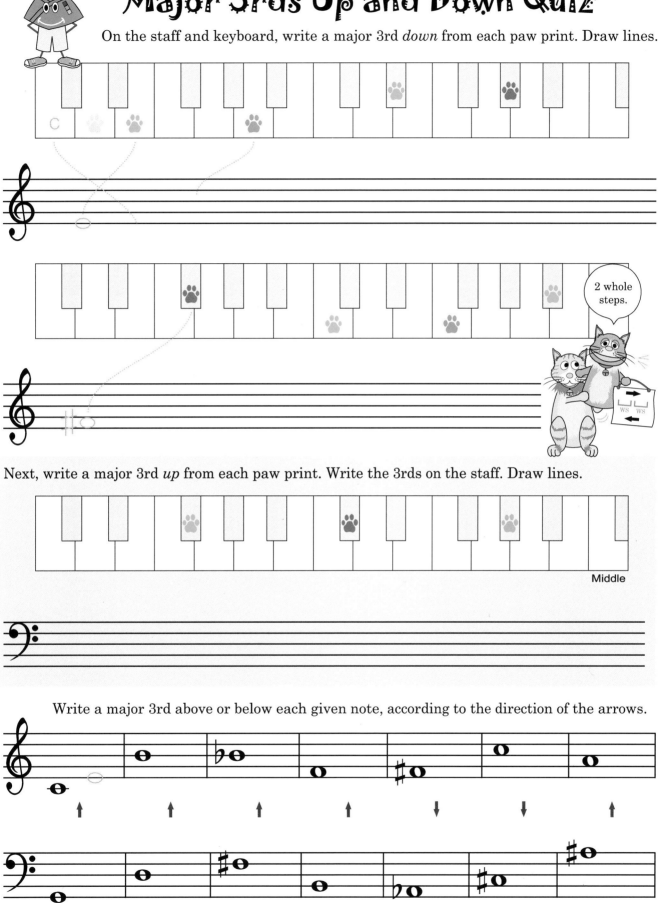

Next, write a major 3rd *up* from each paw print. Write the 3rds on the staff. Draw lines.

Write a major 3rd above or below each given note, according to the direction of the arrows.

Minor 3rds Up & Down Quiz

On the staff and keyboard, write a minor 3rd *down* from each paw print. Draw lines.

It's the same distance, up or down.

WS   HS

Next, write minor 3rds *up* from each paw print. Write the 3rds on the staff too. Draw lines.

Middle

Write a minor 3rd above or below each given note, according to the direction of the arrows.

How Can a 4th be Perfect?

Trace the gray brackets and text. How many cats are there between the red paw prints? _____

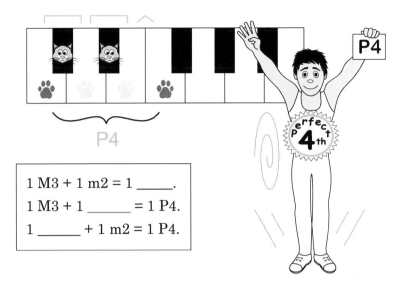

1 M3 + 1 m2 = 1 _____.
1 M3 + 1 _____ = 1 P4.
1 _____ + 1 m2 = 1 P4.

The red paw prints span a perfect 4th, or P4. This perfect 4th spans

_____ whole steps plus _____ half step. In other words, this perfect 4th spans

a major 3rd plus a m_____ 2nd.
A perfect 4th is one half step

larger than a major _____.

We never say that a 4th is major or minor. Instead, we say 4ths are *perfect*. The symbol for perfect 4th is P4.

P4 means p_____ _____.

Every perfect 4th spans 4 notes, known as a tetrachord. A tetrachord contains _____ notes. Below, each set of colored boxes shows a P4 tetrachord. Name the keys. Use adjacent alphabet letters. Draw square and V brackets.

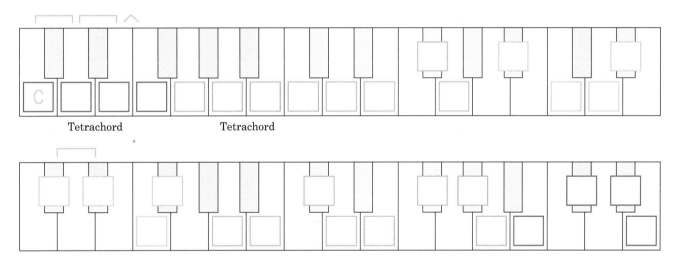

Tetrachord   Tetrachord

Next, name the keys to show the tetrachords. Draw square and V brackets.
Write P4 under each perfect 4th. Write each P4 on the staff. Draw lines.

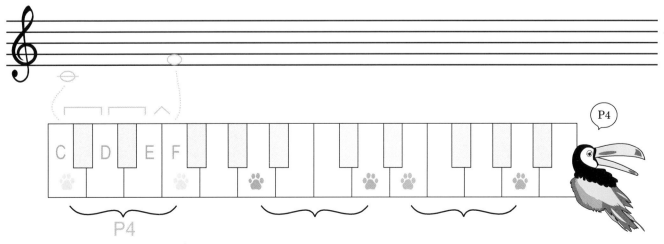

Doctor Mozart Music Theory Workbook, Level 2B.   © MMVIII, MMXII Machiko and Paul Christopher Musgrave.   Published by April Avenue Music.   www.DoctorMozart.com   800 567-8878

Perfect 5ths

Trace these brackets.

C D E F   F G C D E F G

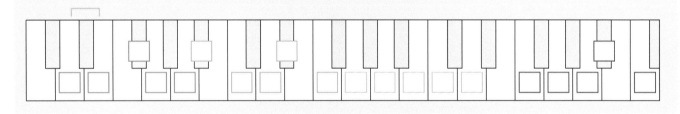

A perfect 4th   +   1 whole step   =   a perfect 5th.

A perfect 5th is one w_____ step larger than a perfect 4th.

P5 is the symbol for perfect 5th.

Trace the brackets on the keyboard.

Each set of colored boxes shows a P5. Name the keys. Use adjacent alphabet letters. Draw square and V brackets.

At right, circle each group of brackets that represents a P5.

A perfect 5th spans 5 alphabet letters.

In a P5, the whole and half steps can be in any order, but they must add up to 3½ steps. Circle each group of brackets that makes a P5.

Next, each colored box is the bottom note of a P5. Name the white keys spanned by each P5. Draw brackets. They will not be in the usual order.

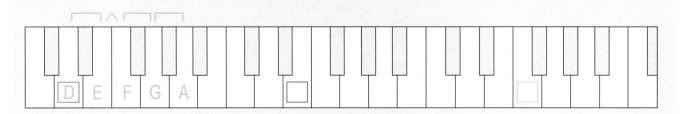

D E F G A

Doctor Mozart Music Theory Workbook, Level 2B.   © MMVIII, MMXII Machiko and Paul Christopher Musgrave.   Published by April Avenue Music.   www.DoctorMozart.com   800 567-8878

Harmonic & Melodic Intervals

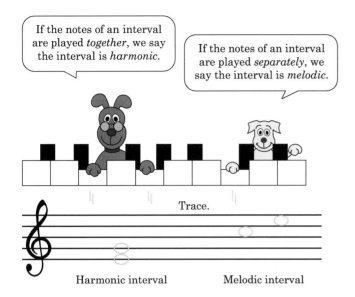

If the notes of an interval are played *together*, we say the interval is *harmonic*.

If the notes of an interval are played *separately*, we say the interval is *melodic*.

Trace.

Harmonic interval   Melodic interval

When writing a harmonic 2nd, do not allow the notes to overlap. Instead, write the notes very close together. Look at these examples:

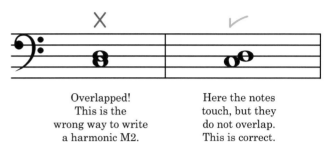

Overlapped! This is the wrong way to write a harmonic M2.

Here the notes touch, but they do not overlap. This is correct.

Name these harmonic intervals. Draw lines to the keyboard.

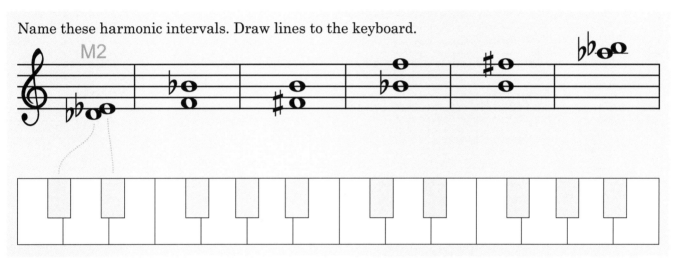

Above each given note, write the harmonic interval indicated. Draw lines to the keyboard.

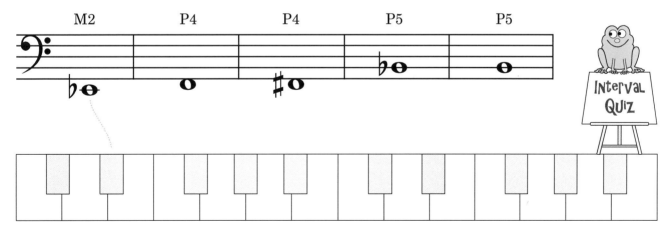

Write the correct clef in each bar to make each interval a perfect 4th.

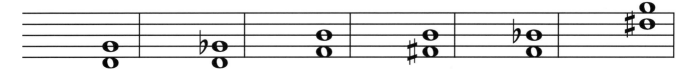

Doctor Mozart Music Theory Workbook, Level 2B.   © MMVIII, MMXII Machiko and Paul Christopher Musgrave.   Published by April Avenue Music.   www.DoctorMozart.com 800 567-8878

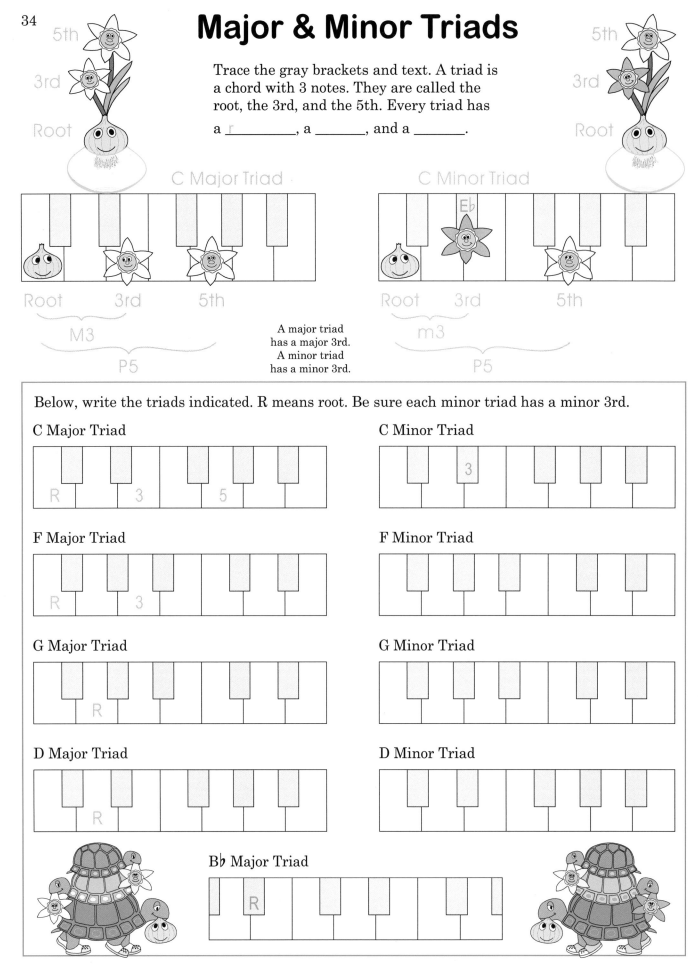

Major & Minor Triads

Trace the gray brackets and text. A triad is a chord with 3 notes. They are called the root, the 3rd, and the 5th. Every triad has a r_____, a _____, and a _____.

A major triad has a major 3rd.
A minor triad has a minor 3rd.

Below, write the triads indicated. R means root. Be sure each minor triad has a minor 3rd.

C Major Triad

C Minor Triad

F Major Triad

F Minor Triad

G Major Triad

G Minor Triad

D Major Triad

D Minor Triad

B♭ Major Triad

Doctor Mozart Music Theory Workbook, Level 2B.   © MMVIII, MMXII Machiko and Paul Christopher Musgrave.   Published by April Avenue Music.   www.DoctorMozart.com   800 567-8878

Tonic, Subdominant & Dominant

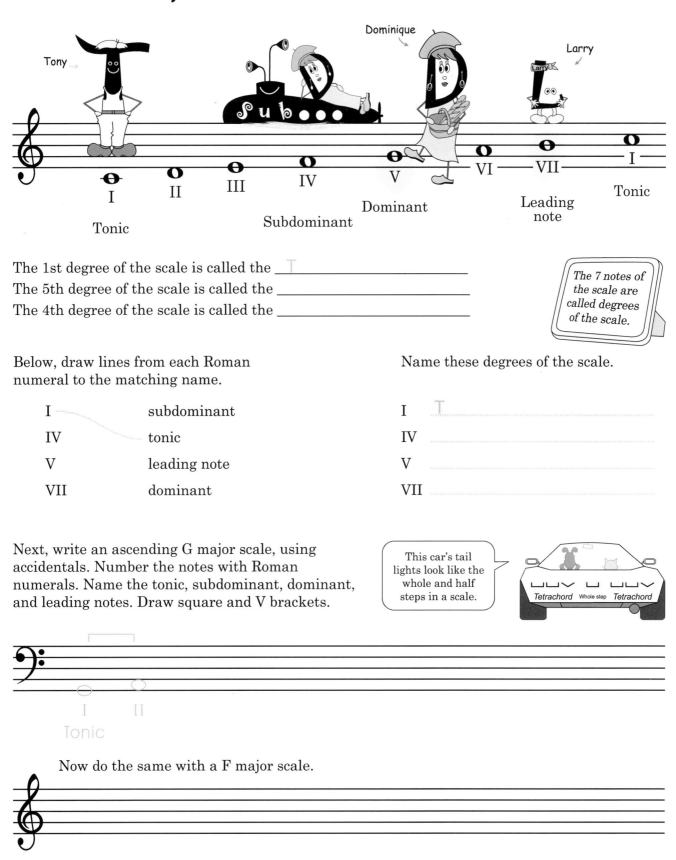

The 1st degree of the scale is called the ___T_____

The 5th degree of the scale is called the _____

The 4th degree of the scale is called the _____

The 7 notes of the scale are called degrees of the scale.

Below, draw lines from each Roman numeral to the matching name.

I .... subdominant

IV .... tonic

V   leading note

VII   dominant

Name these degrees of the scale.

I ___T_____

IV _____

V _____

VII _____

Next, write an ascending G major scale, using accidentals. Number the notes with Roman numerals. Name the tonic, subdominant, dominant, and leading notes. Draw square and V brackets.

This car's tail lights look like the whole and half steps in a scale.

Tetrachord   Whole step   Tetrachord

I   II

Tonic

Now do the same with a F major scale.

The 7 notes of the scale are called ___d_____ of the scale.

Roman numerals are often written with a stroke across the top and bottom.

Doctor Mozart Music Theory Workbook, Level 2B.   © MMVIII, MMXII Machiko and Paul Christopher Musgrave.   Published by April Avenue Music.   www.DoctorMozart.com   800 567-8878

Dominant & Subdominant Triads

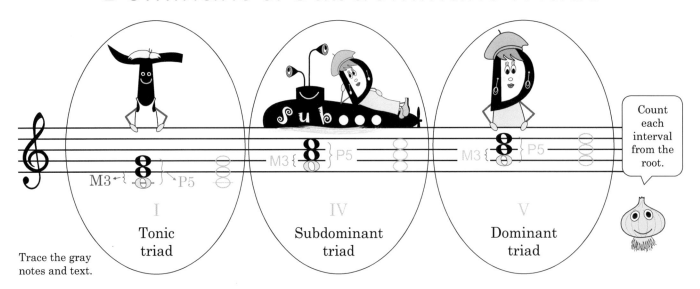

Trace the gray
notes and text.

Tonic
triad

Subdominant
triad

Dominant
triad

Count
each
interval
from the
root.

The chords shown above are the primary triads of the C major scale. They are on I, IV, and V.

The primary triads are on I, IV, and ___ in every scale.

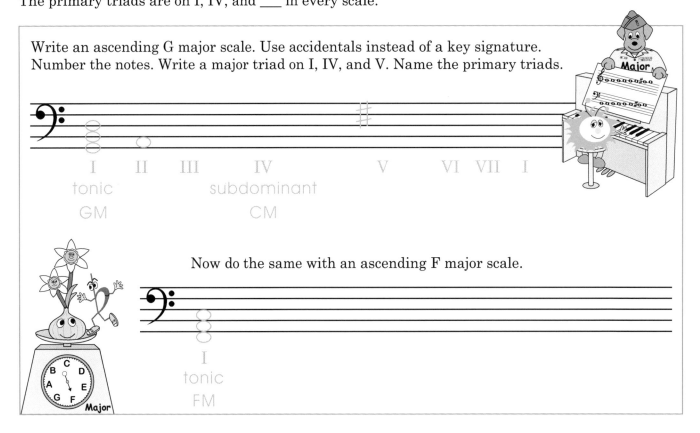

Write an ascending G major scale. Use accidentals instead of a key signature.
Number the notes. Write a major triad on I, IV, and V. Name the primary triads.

I   II   III   IV   V   VI   VII   I
tonic   subdominant
GM   CM

Now do the same with an ascending F major scale.

I
tonic
FM

Write the correct Roman numeral under each triad.

In the C major scale.   In the F major scale.   In the G major scale.

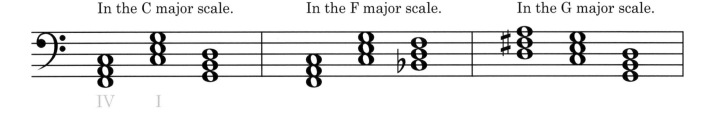

IV   I

Write a single rest at each X to complete the bars. Number the beats.

Write the correct clef for each group of primary triads.

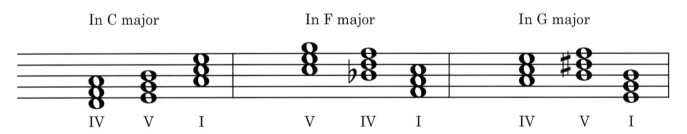

Write Roman numerals in the blanks to match each triad with the scales listed below it.
If there is no correct answer, write an X.

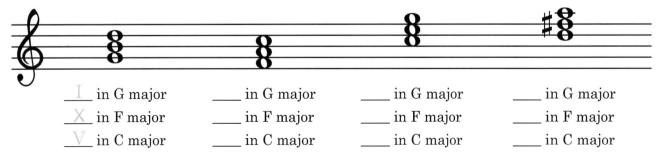

_I_ in G major   ____ in G major   ____ in G major   ____ in G major

_X_ in F major   ____ in F major   ____ in F major   ____ in F major

_V_ in C major   ____ in C major   ____ in C major   ____ in C major

Expert Review

Write the correct clef on each staff to
make every interval either an m3 or P5.

Which
clef?

Which
clef?

Next, name the intervals. Is every minor 3rd followed by a major 3rd? _____

M3   m3

Make two grand staffs, each with a different time signature. Fill some bars with any notes
and rests you like. Include some 2nds, 3rds, 4ths, and 5ths. Also include some eighth rests.
Write some of the musical terms and signs you have learned too. Number the beats.

Congratulations!

Certificate of Achievement

_____
Student name

Now that you have completed
Doctor Mozart Music Theory
Level 2B, you are
ready for Level 2C.

Teacher _____

Date _____

Dr. Mozart

You are ready for Level 2C!

You have learned about:

- Da capo & Dal segno
- Eighth rests
- 2/8, 3/8, and 4/8 time
- White key accidentals
- Major & minor 2nds and 3rds
- Perfect 4ths and 5ths
- Major and minor triads.
- Primary triads in C, F, & G major

You are simply amazing!

See you in the next book!

CPSIA information can be obtained
at www.ICGtesting.com
Printed in the USA
LVIC081102230413
330484LV00003B